THE
RETURN
OF A
PEOPLE

PRAYERS AND DECLARATIONS

DR. B. DWAYNE HARDIN

The Return of a People is a book of prayers taken directly from the scriptures. There were multiple versions used in this book that include:

King James Version
New King James Version
The Message Bible
New International Version
Tree of Live Version

The scriptures used were either a direct quote or a paraphrased version of the text. Most often shifted to read from the 1st person, deeply personalized for honest expression, and internalized with the understanding that it is prayer and declaration for an entire nation, though it is an extreme personal prayer of return.

The personality of these prayers and declarations are not limited to what is written but provided for the sake of context and direction.

PRAISE FOR *THE RETURN*

Apostle Dwayne Hardin has produced a prayer tool that is both informative and applicable. There has been a tremendous draught as it pertains to active actual prayer in the church. There is a wonderful move of the Holy Spirit in the world and in America, and part of this move of God is the restoration of prayer. Prayer is a science and an art.

Apostle Hardin has presented us with a tool to encourage intercessors to direct their prayers towards God restoring and returning what was lost. These prayers are apostolic and prophetic declarations, decrees, and confessions for God to return to His people what was stolen by the demonic world.

These "prayers of return" will enrich your prayer experience and enable your prayers to be more impactful. I pray that God will *return* all that you've lost and *return* what has been hidden. God bless you.

Bishop Tudor Bismark | Harare, Zimbabwe

In this work, *The Return of a People*, the prophetic voice of Apostle B. Dwayne Hardin has released a much-needed clarion call to the body of Christ. Every time God chooses to recall us back to truth, He uses someone from that particular time or environment. I believe that like John, who was exiled to the isle of Patmos, Hardin has been caught up in the Spirit for such a time as this to release this body of work to the global body of believers.

This call is necessary if we are to properly return to apostolic distribution, as he states, which is the job of the church and not the government. God has always provided His people with a pattern, and the patterns of this work follow an awakening to uncompromised truths that will not collapse. He calls us back into the race where the playing grounds are equal, and the result is fruitfulness. We know that we can't keep doing what we've done in the past, and this work challenges us to do, think and act better.

I highly recommend this book for the seasoned saint as well as the novice. It will awaken you to truths that are necessary to overturn these world systems.

Bishop Yvonne Jones | Founder of Covenant Ministries International; International Bishop of Women: Kingdom Connection Fellowship International

The Return of a People is a book in the order of John Bunyan's *Pilgrims Progress*, which carves a clearly laid roadmap for how to cure the spiritual and social ills of America and the greater body of Christ. It helps to reframe the proper application of righteousness and justice by addressing the spiritual and cultural inequities that are common with all humans.

I highly recommend this powerful book for people who are interested in real Kingdom solutions to today's social and cultural narratives that have us at each other's throats. May there be in America, and around the globe, a "return of a people" to the ancient Judeo-Christian foundations that produced the longest lasting constitution in the history of the world, and a land of unparalleled opportunities famously known as the "American Dream".

Dr. Francis Myles | Author of *The Order of Melchizedek* CEO, Francis Myles International

In reading *The Return of a People* I was illuminated, convicted, and pressed toward a strategy of action for truth. Dr. Hardin is one of the greatest minds in the kingdom of God I have ever met. I was moved by his revelation of wrestling with the Jacob inside each of us; but his insight on racism needs to be heard by every White, Black, and Hispanic, as well as all other races in America.

It's one thing to scream at the darkness, but it's quite another to have the Godly wisdom to challenge the evil paradigms that divide us. He has identified solutions that could honestly bring America back to God and *justice*. Righteousness and justice are the only salvation for this great country of ours.

Every person needs to understand Dr. Hardin's wisdom in calling out the abortion epidemic for what it is— a satanic strategy to limit, cripple and eventually destroy our black brothers and sisters.

For 17 years I worked with my uncle to build the largest cross-cultural church in America. We had 7500 black members and 7500 white members. I am always moved when I hear a "voice of hope" challenging demonic world systems with the truth that can bring deliverance to God's people of all colors.

You must read this book over and over. Let this book become part of your DNA. Make the declarations and pray the prayers that this author has given you. Then, and only then, can we sing the old Black spiritual, "Free at last! Free at last! Thank God Almighty, we are free at last!"

Bishop Duane Swilley | Founder of Duane Swilley Ministries, Avi's House, and Dreamnation

The timeliness of this prophetic prayer masterpiece could not have been disseminated within the kingdom of God at a more propitious juncture in our history. As I always say, "Prayer is the only legitimate vehicle between Heaven and Earth that enables the deployment of God's power here in the earth realm, relative to establishing His kingdom here in real-time."

For a people to return to their original place of inheritance and dominion, as mandated by God, they must first return to a place of prayer with God. Apostle B. Dwayne Hardin has unequivocally downloaded targeted and strategic instructions from the mind of God; and as a result, these directives will provide the divine enablement to reorient us toward our original place of leadership, influence, and magnetism as a people within this global village.

The Return of a People is a book with a mission to matriculate us to a place of kingdom mastery through the legitimate use of the technology of prayer. As you journey through this book, you are subscribing to a kingdom movement in real-time that is supported by a divine mandate that will shift your life into a sustainable place of Prayer-Power!

Dr. Jason Renville | UN AMB - ECOSOC - NGO & HRR Representative, ICN World Civility Statesman, PVSA Agent, Nelson Mandela Peace Award Recipient

What a thought-provoking delivery Apostle B. Dwayne Hardin gives to us in this presentation. It's a rehearsing of Jeremiah 6:16 which says, "...Stand ye in the ways, and see, and ask for the old paths, where is the good way, and walk therein, and ye shall find rest for your souls...". It's a return to the ancient paths. As he pens, we walk together to investigate landmarks and demarcations of places and time as our hearts are tied deeper to God in prayer, coming out with treasures.

In our world, we constantly examine problems that cause us to overlook solutions that are right in front of our faces. Simple, yet powerful. Within these pages, we see answers. Not only do we recover and discover answers; we become the answer. Henceforth, if we are not answering a problem, we in-turn *are* the problem. Thank you, Dr. Hardin, for pouring your life into this work.

Dr. Will Thornton | *Bishop, King of Kings Global*

DEDICATION

This book is dedicated to the memory of my spiritual father, Bishop Norman L. Wagner. There was no one else like him, and there never will be. He was the wisest man I knew, and I miss him greatly, but I will always feel his push, hear his counsel, and value the impact he's made on my life. Thank you for being the man that believed in me when rejection was continually lurking, for picking me up after falling, and for covering me when I was exposed. Bishop, I dedicate this to you!

I also want to dedicate this book to my grandmothers, Martha Jean Eldridge and Sarah Lee Cross. I sat at both your doors and listened to you pray. Your persistent reach for God kept me through some of the lowest moments of my life. I love and miss you!

ACKNOWLEDGMENTS

I would like to acknowledge those who pushed me to complete this book, directly or indirectly. Those who read this book when it was grammatically incorrect and needed editing. Those who stayed on me when my schedule overwhelmed me.

To the church that I am so blessed to lead, The Embassy in Atlanta, GA: Thank you so much for trusting my voice. When I take a journey with Yah, you get on board and take that journey with me.

I have the best mother and God-mother. Thank you for being the epitome of virtuous women. Both of you have been so classy, kept the bar high, and loved me gracefully. I'm so honored you call me *son*. To my mother, Anner Hardin, and God-mother, Bishop Pat McKinstry, I love you!

I want to acknowledge every educator that framed my curiosity for truth, knowledge and understanding. You taught me to think, remain balanced, observe history, and focus on the details. Thank you!

To all my spiritual sons, daughters, and mentees: You push me to new dimensions no matter what. You're Black, White, Brown, American, Latin, African, Indian, European, and it does not matter—I love you all! I am honored by your honor, trust, and love.

I acknowledge my children, grandchildren and God-children. God gave you me, and I plan to give you a legacy of honor, grace, and wealth. You are chosen.

To the descendants of the Atlantic Slave Trade. Our time has come, our redemption is here. Let us *return* and lead our children in the ways of Yahweh, our God. We are called by His name.

FOREWORD

by Leo S. Lewis, Sr.

Apostle Hardin challenges us to shed old wineskins that are brittle museums of old thought in exchange for new possibilities of Christ-mindedness.

Unapologetically, he speaks to the soul of the nation while plowing the dark and rocky subconscious mind of Black, White, and Jewish subcultures. His poignant instructive, combative, and accusatory systematic diatribe, ultimately leads to the possibility of redemption—if one is graced to be instructed by naked truth.

Mediocrity is always a formidable foe to one's pursuit of excellence of virtue. What does one do when attempting to move into one's future—only to be confronted by a regrettable past?

Apostle Hardin, in a loving but strident manner, instructs us personally, culturally, and nationally to wrestle with the characters we play, as in theater, to become persons of character.

We find that in solitude and aloneness we become, through the wrestle, "my best me".

Come join me as I wrestle.

INTRODUCTION

And Jacob was left **alone**, and **there** (alone); **wrestled a man** with him. --Genesis 32:24

And Now We Wrestle

Let me begin by requesting that you rest your traditional theological thought patterns to allow your paradigms to be shifted. The Bible is specific to state that *Jacob was alone, or by himself.* This place in Genesis 32:24, where Jacob was all alone, is the site of this wrestling match.

Was it an Angel he wrestled? Well, that doesn't make sense considering the size, strength, and might of the angelic beings we study in the scriptures; and to do it until the breaking of the day? I do not think that would be possible.

Was Jacob wrestling with God (Yah)? Logically speaking, if he couldn't handle an angel, God is out of the picture. Please consider that the man he wrestled was himself. Yes, this was not a physical match, but a mental match that Jacob had to fight to discover himself as Israel.

I submit to you that Jacob *(the trickster, the heel grabber)* was wrestling with his god-self *(Israel).* Consider it a battle between the divine and the flesh— the original intent of God for him versus his own fleshly, crooked approach to destiny.

There is always a better *you* in you, and to put that *you* in the seat of authority of your life, you must be transformed by the renewing of your mind. You will have to fight mentally and allow purpose to cripple old thoughts, patterns, and vices.

America

America is in a sort of wrestling match right now. Babylon is fighting for control of the soul of America, a country of principle, law, and order. A place where you discover freedom in a different way than any other country in the world. A place where people can hate you, yet they cannot stop you from fulfilling your purpose.

America is a place where you can dream, wake up and build that dream. A place where Judea-Christian principles are all throughout the constitution, but every other people group are welcomed here, even if they have different beliefs. The American experiment is a beautiful one that has needed tweaking, healing, and change, but still a beautiful one, nonetheless.

Everyone wants a to get in on the American race. The race for freedom, wealth, and opportunity. Most come here unmoved by the potential racism and bigotry that can plague this land, they look beyond towards the prize of freedom, wealth, and opportunity.

People of all ethnicities break the laws to get here. They work for pennies on the dollar simply to be in America. They work and work—sending their earned income to their homeland in hopes of reuniting with their families.

It is noted that while some have been able to jump into the race, others were brought here in ships to work the land for those who saw the opportunity to get in the race. Racism is rooted in this and should be etymologically understood as a term birthed from leaving a group of people out of that opportunity.

Racism

Slavery was the mechanism that built America, but the mistreatment of Jim Crow laws sustained the ideology of racism. It totally kept Black America out of the race of *Equal Opportunity*. Now racism is basically an over-used term, designed to incite emotions that translate into votes needed to erect political agendas that never produce resolute policy. The real goal is to infiltrate the constitution with Babylonian philosophy.

So, we find ourselves as a nation in a wrestling match for equal opportunity, and Baal has jumped into the mindset of this country, causing us to receive all kinds of idolatry, worship, and debauchery. We then find it expedient to simply crowd everything together, never resolving issues, but benching them as a way of maintaining seats of power while pointing to *someday* we will get this done.

We are wrestling with old paradigms, and trickery that's enslaved and mistreated purpose. Then there is the fight for *righteousness and justice* versus the wicked systems of Baal. Very few want to tell the truth, thus making way for every kind of evil.

Righteousness and Justice

Righteous **and** Justice is the civil rights system of the Kingdom of God. It is not discriminating and is available to everyone no matter what. It gives value to every life, acknowledges God as the giver of that life and indiscriminately provides opportunity.

We wrestle with the Biblical truth of Righteousness and Justice because it is principled; it points to a standard of truth, and it instills conscience. Babylon hates God-consciousness because it can lead to conviction and produce delivering repentance.

Righteousness and Justice is not a religious concept, rather it is societal. It is provided for the dignity and morality of all people. It says that all people need justice, yet there is a way to do it righteously, where conscience is not eliminated.

Morality cannot be legislated, and for a while the church thought that to be possible. Legislated morality is forced righteousness, and it would take away the free will of people to serve Yah (God) with purity of heart and willingness of person.

Immorality is a much more dangerous topic to consider in legislation. You must never legislate laws empowering immoral living dangerous to generations waiting to be released in the sperm of the immoral. Yes, you have the choice to be immoral, but you do not have the right to self-impose it upon those coming behind you.

Legislation

Legislation of the unrighteous thing is what diminishes the power of truth. It is what redefines right as wrong, and wrong as right. It produces laws that silences the prophetic voice of consciousness and volumizes the sound of Baal; therefore, justice will be distorted, and freedom for some will produce bondage for others.

The ongoing battle between legalism and lawlessness will rage vehemently until righteousness and justice have reunited as one dependent on each other.

The church hides behind the *anointing* and demand for *righteousness,* but often ignore the hendiadys connection of justice. Righteousness and Justice must go together, because righteousness without justice will produce legalism and the cry for justice alone will result in lawlessness. One without the other will not work.

We know there are issues such as racism, but the onslaught of it is mainly the propaganda of media systems that want control. Willing to cancel out every voice that does not fit their mold.

It's that *crazy racist Trump* and that wall, right?

No! We now see that we need a wall with a door, not only for the people, but for the wicked systems we've allowed to spiritually infiltrate this nation just as Solomon did when he married for peace to avoid war. They brought their gods, and Solomon accommodated them. Sounds like America, huh?

Well, it must be the White man and his toxic masculinity that want all the women as sex toys, black people as slaves, and the homosexuals killed, right?

Yes, that exists as does every other kind of bigotry among all people groups, so let us not fake blindness. That, nonetheless, is also propaganda used to fulfil an agenda as well. There are great people of every ethnicity, but we must also recognize the bad people in each people group.

It's them Black people, right? Running around screaming Black Lives Matter destroying their own communities. We know they were brought here in ships and were enslaved and mistreated, but they need to get over it. They now complain and desire justice, equal rights, and reparations.

No matter what, the fingers keep pointing while wickedness pursues its goal.

The Church

The greatest argument among *Christians* would be that the church has lost its anointing and we do not pray. A large part of that is true; however, I submit once more that this country must be hit in its thigh so that the God-design of the country shows forth and cripples the corruption therein.

Between the years of 2017-2019, I was so prophetically troubled about the state of the church until I felt compelled to call a Summit of leaders from both the *Black* and *White* church. The Summit was to consist of leaders who weren't afraid of a good brotherly fight towards solution and change. It never happened, except in brief conversations of, "yes we need to do this."

We do not need another forgiveness, wash-the-black-man's-feet session. What we need is to *get in there* and wrestle until we figure out how to be brothers and sisters who will not relent in our stand for each other as Believers.

We need to wrestle until we have dealt with our own racism and bigotry, which we cover up with a pseudo type of love—and I'm talking on both sides. Truth is, you have a choice if you want to love me or not, and I the same.

We must stop loosely using love as a non-negotiable and love each other from the purity of our hearts. There is an innate fear of talking bluntly, or approaching the *elephants in the room*; nonetheless, the immediate need to discuss these issues remain.

We need to deal with the abortion issue, racism in the church, and the apparent injustices that deprive entire people groups. We need to quit protecting our seats of authority and use that authority to help people.

Too often the church is making the wrong kind of noise. Furthermore, the noise we make is like a tinkling clanging cymbal because we are fruitless.

You may not like me for this, but there is no other people group terrorized as deeply as Black America, including the Jews. The Holocaust and every other evil attack is horrific, but they cannot compete with the sufferings inflicted on Black America. Nonetheless, there has been a more unified effort, higher degree of documentation and significant amount of funding around the bitter woes of the Ashkenazi and Sephardic Jewish population, and this is not so in Black America.

We have not compiled or properly documented the woes of slavery, the millions of bodies of black Negroes in the sea due to the treacherous ship rides and the devastating lynching's of the KKK. The film industry has not been as favorable to Black America, and our history, for the most part has been wiped away in concert with other powerful organizations. This has created big problems for much needed healing.

It's been more convenient to either cover up this devastating American history, work to destroy the country, or force an entirely different government construct that is empirically proven destructive. The story goes on, but the point is that grave injustices exist.

We need to get together, talk, and stop waiting on the government. Our political leaders have diligently proven to us that they are not the answer.

As Black people, we need to open our scope beyond what we see on social media and television, and raise our own standard following the laws of God. More importantly, we must place a demand on legislative policy. Our protest must be led by men and women of God who are filled with the Spirit of God and not greed.

We need to close the gaps of division among us, and among our brethren. We must see beyond racism, deal with our own bigotry, and build change.

White people... I challenge you to see beyond what is visible through the eyes of judgement. I cannot tell you how many White people feel the need to chastise the condition of the *Black church* or *Black man* without walking one mile with their feet.

On the other hand, Black people need to look at the feet of the White person. You would be increasingly surprised at what you would discover. You might find that their boots were not comfortable, maybe a bit oversized or undersized. You may find that their feet have tread some of the same paths as you.

Incidentally, we may all find that we are not as different as we think we are.

The goal: stop demonizing each other, and wrestle until we are transformed as we renew our minds together.

It's important that we wrestle. *We need to hear your side, and you need to hear our side.* And then we need to follow the example of Yeshua (Jesus) and intentionally lead with apostolic solutions for change, unity, and strength. The systems of this world cannot conquer us if we are together.

One of the times I met with President Donald Trump was intriguing. He walked into the boardroom of Trump Towers, kindly and comfortably as he generously welcomed and greeted nearly 100 Black pastors. He then spoke about the power of the *Christian Church*. He stated that the Church, at large, is numerically strong, and can have any president it wants, *"but you're so divided,"* he stated, *"with all of these denominations and sects".*

Church, we are that house divided against itself. Therefore we have not stood unified. We will not build or come together. We do not share in resources together. We *love* each other, but don't fight for each other. We are not willing to look deeper at history and restore identity. We would rather smooth things over with *the blood.* This must change! We must wrestle a while until we cripple this issue.

The Abortion Issue

Politicians argue for abortion largely because they do not want to spend the necessary money to feed, clothe and educate more people. Here arguments for inconvenience and economic savings take precedence over arguments for human value and human life... Psychiatrists, social workers and doctors often argue for abortion on the basis that the child will grow up mentally and emotionally scarred. But who of us is complete? If incompleteness were the criterion for taking life, we would all be dead. If you can justify abortion on the basis of emotional incompleteness, then your logic could also lead you to killing for other forms of incompleteness — blindness, cripple-ness, old age..."

(Then pro-life) Jesse Jackson, January 1977

Abortion has affected some 60 million helpless lives since 1973, and more than 20 million were Black Americans. In 2018 approximately 2400 babies were aborted daily, with 38% of those being Black while only making up 13-14% of the US population. This means that 456 Hispanic, 840 White, and 912 Black babies were aborted daily, according to Abort73.

Just imagine having 2400 members in your church and you lose over 912 of them overnight all because they were hated, targeted, or manipulated. Be certain, that impact will be devastating and will significantly alter the plans of that church.

Margaret Sanger is one of the most proficient American activists. She actively developed a long-term solution towards her vitriolic disdain of Black people, more specifically as she developed Planned Parenthood. At any time, 30-40% of all black babies are being aborted, diminishing the Black community's growth, wealth, political influence, and overall effectiveness.

Planned Parenthood has admitted the wicked plot of its founder, Sanger, and claims to have changed its values since her death, but nothing is able to leave its origin of creation and survive. Abortions targeting Black babies in the womb is still the driving force of this organization today.

In Georgia, 32.2% of the overall population is Black American. The *Centers for Disease Control (CDC)* statistically report that 62.4% of Georgia's abortions are performed on Black Americans while 24.7% of White women are affected by the same. In the neighboring state of Mississippi, 72% of non-Hispanic Black American babies were aborted.

Public Discourse accurately reports that, *"These abortion numbers have curtailed population increases in the African-American community."* It should be noted that this fact is true throughout the entire US. This crime extends to the death, growth, influence, and productivity of the Black population. This is a crisis of epidemic proportions being swept under the rug and justified for political expedience.

What if the first Black American was aborted before President Obama was ever selected? What if the world's leading economist capable of healing this capitalist system to a place of equitable wealth was never born, but aborted? Just think of the potential police officer who would have been bold enough to stop the heinous murder of George Floyd, but he was aborted.

Margaret Sanger's mission was not only to kill the physical baby, but her goal was also to annihilate the presence, essence, strength, productivity, and ultimate world influence of Black America. The economists, agriculturalist, archaeologists, medical brilliance, educational impact, and spirituality of Black America to this country is what she aimed to abort.

The Jezebel spirit couldn't stand the rise from the ashes of a chosen, durable, and resilient people. That infamous spirit of old is still alive in the form of Jezebel and Ahab.

Yes, the issue of abortion is huge in America—more specifically, Black America. We cannot afford to be lulled to sleep any longer as some of our legislators work tirelessly to implement legislation that provides unlimited abortions. The fight against this should never be considered as moral legislation because morality is a matter of option, free will, and choice.

We have seen a drop in legal abortions, but it is no reason to celebrate, especially since the Biden administration's day one goal was to incentivize and make this crime more attractive. If the product you seek to sell is not selling as you desire, you simply incentivize it with sales, discounts, rebates, and convenience, especially if you are indoctrinated with its outcome.

No Believer should support this, especially with the legislation we have before us now. No matter which party you support, keeping that loyalty is a disgrace when it goes against the heart of God for His people. We must look beyond party affiliation and re-prioritize our standards.

We fight hard with our protests and votes towards saving the lives of our young men and women that are shot in the street by bad policing. We need that same fervor, spirit, and support for the babies in the womb. We need to give them the same opportunity at life, opportunity, and success. We must stop the literal murder of destiny and greatness.

To all who have experienced abortion, please do not see anything as an attack against you. This was done by our enemies, and it has touched millions of lives, directly or indirectly. This should not be read as a cookie cutter solution for all situations regarding abortion either. Though it is opposed, I also understand the plight of many, and hold no condemnation over anyone's head.

This is a real systemic justice that we must not support legislatively, especially where it is propagated through linguistic deception. Once you discover the blatant design, original intent, and strategic funding, it should break your heart.

And, for every preacher who would seek to justify abortion as just, or simply a sin that needs forgiving, you should check what god you are aligned to. The prophets of Baal were true prophets to Baal, and they should not be mistaken as false because they were not aligned with the Most High.

When you do the bidding of Baal, you are now a Prophet of Baal just like the mainstream media. You can twist scripture all you like, but you are not representing God. You cannot make right wrong and wrong right and use God to do so.

Prophetic Sight

The word of the Lord is exactly that, and it should not be mis-handled or unwisely judged.

We have been significantly guilty of delivering a Word from the mouth and heart of God (Yah) intertwined with our opinions, bias, and paradigms. The lens of the prophetic is often smeared with denomination, ethnicity, our background, pride, or doctrines. Prophetically we tend to see and hear differently, but we serve the same God. How is this? How can we be so diametrically opposed when speaking to the same God?

God spoke to me, and said this flaw is because we operate from a realm of opinion and not His heart. We have been prophesying what we see or hear, but rarely from the heart eyes of the Father; therefore, we bear the prophetic fruit of opinion, and not the truth of the Father's heart. So, a *White prophet* sees one thing and the *Black prophet* sees the direct opposite. Then we discount each other's validity because they are not of *my people group.*

A prophet cannot be aligned with anything other than God. Whatever you align your loyalties to will always influence how you think and speak. In turn, Holy Spirit will only be able to speak to that level of your revelation, which will often be contaminated by opinion from un-Godly alignment. You will see, but the lens will be blurred by loyalty to your alliance.

A prophet cannot be blinded by Democrat or Republican perspectives. They must be as the sons of Issachar—aware of the times and seasons, and what must be done in them. The prophetic can no longer be contaminated with limited sight and massive opinion.

We need a good wrestling match. I sincerely believe this.

Socialism Is A Must

Now that I have your attention: the true phraseology should be an *"Apostolic Distribution"*, which is described in Acts, where they had all things in common. *Apostolic Distribution* is not only the proper terminology, but it is the job of the church, not the government.

We do ourselves harm putting our trust in the care of the government. Big government is a controlling force that strips its constituents of liberty and opportunity and builds an addictive dependency upon its system of handouts. The Kingdom of God in operation does the opposite and will always empower your life.

The Kingdom is available to us here in the earth. It is what Yeshua (Jesus) came to implement, and this Kingdom produces life. Yeshua said, I have come that you might have life, and live that life in abundance of peace, joy, love, and substance.

Azusa Street Revival

Azusa was that hour for the church; however, the Assemblies of God and several other denominations were formed because they would not follow a Black leader. So, they had that same Black leader, Bishop Charles H. Mason, ordain them for the sanctioning of this devastating church split. This weakened the church immediately and diminished its ability to impact society.

The resources that would have destroyed the division of color were consumed at the onset of cowardness and caused the two powerhouses to divide. Can you imagine what we could have done together? We did not wrestle, and now we war.

If we wrestle, Esau will not kill us.

Truth Revelations

There are many revelations of truth that are coming forth. People groups will discover their identity—something that has been hidden, stolen, and replaced for centuries, but God is revealing it in this hour.

If we don't wrestle now, we will not be able to handle these truths, and the political structures of our day will further enslave our minds with their anti-Christ systems.

I hear the Lord saying, this is the hour that there will be significant unveilings from the hidden places in the Vatican. Just as the injustice of child molestation and rape have been revealed, so will many other things. I will cause them to unlock the gates to show what's behind the walls of secrecy that has destroyed My people, and the world will freely see as technology enters the forbidden places.

Pictures will reveal what money, power and intention has hidden. For this is that hour—the hour I unlock the hidden treasures, says God.

Using this Book

This book is a book of prayer rooted in the scriptures, it is designed to open perspective, restore identity, shift paradigms, and develop unity. The goal is to trigger a desire to return to the ways and thoughts of Yah (The Lord).

As you pray these prayers, you are praying scripture, and therefore the heart of Yahweh concerning your life and His will. The scripture anchor is Torah rooted, but the writings of the Prophets, New Testament and Psalms are all sprinkled heavily within.

The prayers are meant to be aligning, while the introduction was to be insightfully awakening.

Upon leaving his uncle Laban, Jacob grabbed his family and earnings, and he left. Through a series of experiences and his time with God, he was driven to make some things right. He is returning to his brother Esau, who he knows is upset with him.

Jacob had been riddled with a life of trickery and deceit from his uncle and his brother. To move forward from this, he heads to his brother to make amends. Along the way he has this mental warfare with himself, wrestling all night long until he prevails and discovers a better version of himself.

He would not have been successful in his return without the success of that mental wrestling match with himself. Israel lived as Jacob until he was ready to fight for Israel.

As you return, you will have to fight in prayer, worship, and study. You will have to master forgiveness, so that you are not mastered by un-forgiveness. You will have to journal so that you can look back and see how much progress you have made.

No matter who you are, please read and pray these prayers and declarations as a united people. Conclude that you are a part of that *coat of many colors*. Most importantly, above your genealogy, acknowledge that the sacrifice of Yeshua brings us together through one blood, His blood.

Finally, a people without identity are doomed, yet when you discover who you are you lose inferiority. Also, do not forget that it doesn't posture you to have superiority over others, but it gives assignment and purpose to identity. Allow the Most High to reveal Himself to you, and I guarantee you will find yourself.

Last, within these pages are prayers intended to usher in the true Spirit of the Most High, declaring many of His promises, making ready the hearts and minds. Read them aloud, meditate on them, journal about them, share them with others, but above all, posture yourself for Him to move in your life.

THE RETURN OF A PEOPLE
PART ONE

Father, I declare that we, Your people, return unto Your statutes and Your ways. We agree to observe and do all of Your commandments, and we ask that You return unto us your people who have been enslaved, mistreated and humbled.

Pray & Declare

_____

_____

_____

_____

_____

_____

_____

_____

_____

_____

_____

_____

We thank You that the end of a period has come, and we begin a new chapter; but we need a renewed mind, and Your deliverance from an enslaved mentality.

>> Pray & Declare <<

_____

_____

_____

_____

_____

_____

_____

_____

_____

_____

_____

_____

_____

We thank You that the curse of the law has no dominion over us. And because of Your grace, we can return to Your highest thoughts and ways. The curse of sin and death can no longer block our access.

>> Pray & Declare <<

_____
_____
_____
_____
_____
_____
_____
_____
_____
_____
_____
_____

Though we are a people once held down, we recognize that it was because of our own disobedience that we were sentenced to this degree of humiliation. We now return and take full responsibility.

⟫ Pray & Declare ⟪

_____

_____

_____

_____

_____

_____

_____

_____

_____

_____

_____

_____

We know that no enemy can
stand against your chosen, and
we are Your chosen.

Pray & Declare

Once again, Father, place us on high, above all the nations of the world. We arise and shine! For our light is come, and the glory of the Lord is risen upon us. Thank You for turning your face towards us, to favor and reposition us.

⟫ Pray & Declare ⟪

_____

_____

_____

_____

_____

_____

_____

_____

_____

_____

_____

We declare and walk in the promised blessings that come down and surround us because we have set out hearts to respond to Your voice, Lord (Yah). This is our day of liberation.

⟫ Pray & Declare ⟪

_____

_____

_____

_____

_____

_____

_____

_____

_____

_____

_____

_____

Restore the blessing upon Your people: Bless us inside the city and in the countries whereto we have been scattered.

Pray & Declare

Blessings be upon our children, and their children, throughout millennia.

Pray & Declare

_____

_____

_____

_____

_____

_____

_____

_____

_____

_____

_____

Bless the crops of our land and the foods we eat. Free us of all sickness and disease attached to the curse of slave diets. We return to Your way, Lord (Yah).

⟫ Pray & Declare ⟪

_____

_____

_____

_____

_____

_____

_____

_____

_____

_____

_____

_____

_____

_____

Bless our livestock, financial opportunities, businesses, investments, real estate and endeavors. We declare perpetual multiplication, expansion and profit from generation to generation.

>>> Pray & Declare <<<

_____

_____

_____

_____

_____

_____

_____

_____

_____

_____

_____

_____

_____

Blessings be upon the land You return to us. We will build cities, produce order, plant gardens and operate peacefully in abundance as we protect our borders.

Pray & Declare

Blessings be upon our baskets. Make them sturdy and able to handle the harvest of the reapers so that we don't lose any of our harvest.

>> Pray & Declare <<

_____

_____

_____

_____

_____

_____

_____

_____

_____

_____

_____

_____

_____

The basket of the stock market, real-estate, operating machinery, our companies, etc. will always be favorable and sturdy towards us.

>> Pray & Declare <<

_____

_____

_____

_____

_____

_____

_____

_____

_____

_____

_____

_____

_____

_____

The harvest will no longer enter the front door and exit the back, but will circulate in great multiplication before exiting, and only to serve as seed for another return.

>> **Pray & Declare** <<

_____

_____

_____

_____

_____

_____

_____

_____

_____

_____

_____

_____

Our nets will not break; our baskets are deep and sturdy.

Pray & Declare

_____

_____

_____

_____

_____

_____

_____

_____

_____

_____

_____

_____

Bless our kneading bowl (bread bowl). We will never have an interruption in the supplies that feed, increase and prosper us. Your blessing is upon us as we come in and go out.

>> **Pray & Declare** <<

_____

_____

_____

_____

_____

_____

_____

_____

_____

_____

_____

_____

THE RETURN OF A PEOPLE
PART TWO

The enemies of our minds, and the system that has attacked us, are now defeated. They came in strength united as one, but now they are weakened, scattered and fleeing seven ways.

>> **Pray & Declare** <<

_____

_____

_____

_____

_____

_____

_____

_____

_____

_____

_____

_____

Yah (Lord), order a blessing on our places of productivity, storage of fruitfulness and our workplaces of creativity, learning, invention and manufacturing.

 Pray & Declare

_____

_____

_____

_____

_____

_____

_____

_____

_____

_____

Bless us in the land You are giving to us as well as the land You are restoring to us.

Pray & Declare

_____

_____

_____

_____

_____

_____

_____

_____

_____

_____

_____

_____

Set us apart as Your holy people, distinguishable by Your great blessings, favor and glory.

Pray & Declare

Form us as holy unto You, just as You have promised us. For we will obey you, keep Your commands and live as You have shown us.

▶▶ Pray & Declare ◀◀

_____

_____

_____

_____

_____

_____

_____

_____

_____

_____

_____

_____

As we awaken, Father, be merciful unto us and grace us through this process of returning to Your statutes and ways, which are given to align and set us high above the earth in our thoughts and ways.

 Pray & Declare

_____

_____

_____

_____

_____

_____

_____

_____

_____

_____

_____

Teach us to live the way You show us, and not according to our feelings, emotions and idol influences.

>>> **Pray & Declare** <<<

_____

_____

_____

_____

_____

_____

_____

_____

_____

_____

_____

_____

_____

_____

We arise to our place where all people groups see us living under the name of The Most High God (Yah), and are respectfully in awe of You and us--because You are the God who keeps His Word unto His people.

>>> Pray & Declare <<<

_____

_____

_____

_____

_____

_____

_____

_____

_____

_____

_____

_____

_____

Lavish us, oh God, with good things: Children from our womb. Forgive us for the sins of our wombs. Increase offspring from our animals--our beasts of productivity--the crops of our land, portfolios and business investments. The same land You promised our ancestors, give unto us.

》》 Pray & Declare 《《

_____

_____

_____

_____

_____

_____

_____

_____

_____

_____

_____

_____

Father, throw open the doors, windows, portals and sky vaults. Open Your bounteous store, the heavens, to provide rain on schedule. Bless all undertakings that unify Your people, educate, equip and empower us. Undertakings that return us to Your way and prosper us.

>> Pray & Declare <<

_____

_____

_____

_____

_____

_____

_____

_____

_____

_____

_____

_____

We declare we are the lenders
and not the borrowers,
creditor to many nations, and
debtor to none. Our financial
stability as a people isn't shaken.

>> **Pray & Declare** <<

_____

_____

_____

_____

_____

_____

_____

_____

_____

_____

_____

_____

_____

Our lending institutions are restored to us, and operate in class and dignity.

Pray & Declare

Our returns on investment (ROI) yield much return, and the currency of our nation circulates multiple times internally before ever touching the hands of other nations.

>> Pray & Declare <<

_____

_____

_____

_____

_____

_____

_____

_____

_____

_____

_____

_____

_____

We are Your people who return to You. Restore us, Lord of Hosts.

⋙ Pray & Declare ⋘

_____
_____
_____
_____
_____
_____
_____
_____
_____
_____
_____
_____
_____
_____

Open our eyes to no longer walk in deception, systems of false promises, deception and perpetual declination. Free our minds, Father, and turn on the switch that immediately restores light, sight, mental perception and fortitude.

>>> **Pray & Declare** <<<

_____

_____

_____

_____

_____

_____

_____

_____

_____

_____

_____

_____

_____

Remove every president, senator, representative, legislator, judge, pastor or community leader who misrepresents Your civil-thoughts and ways regarding us.

>>> **Pray & Declare** <<<

_____

_____

_____

_____

_____

_____

_____

_____

_____

_____

_____

_____

Raise up our Joshua's, Caleb's, Samuel's, David's, Solomon's, Esther's, Josiah's, Nathan's, Paul's, John's, Mary's, Rahab's, Chenaniah's, Bathsheba's--place and replace, oh God. Give us leaders whom You lead!

>> Pray & Declare <<

_____

_____

_____

_____

_____

_____

_____

_____

_____

_____

_____

_____

Make us the head. Restore our headship so that the body may properly function. Put us back into position so that we will make our contribution to the earth.

>>> **Pray & Declare** <<<

_____

_____

_____

_____

_____

_____

_____

_____

_____

_____

_____

_____

The tail isn't our positioning. We must return to the head so that aptitude, conscience, forgiveness and grace can flow just as Katrina overtook NOLA. We drop our levees and move in Your flow.

❯❯ Pray & Declare ❮❮

_____

_____

_____

_____

_____

_____

_____

_____

_____

_____

_____

We return to the top and will never visit the bottom again. We don't belong there, and therefore distort the purposes of those who do. Seat us where we belong. We return, Father.

>> **Pray & Declare** <<

_____

_____

_____

_____

_____

_____

_____

_____

_____

_____

_____

_____

Restore leaders to this great people, un-blinded by cultural deceptions, greed of position, religious folly and identity propaganda--men and women who will speak clearly, strategize successfully and build systemically according to Your thoughts and ways.

》》 Pray & Declare 《《

_____

_____

_____

_____

_____

_____

_____

_____

_____

_____

_____

_____

_____

_____

Give us generational teachers who will establish our way, so that we will not deviate to the right or to the left of any of Your commands.

Pray & Declare

_____
_____
_____
_____
_____
_____
_____
_____
_____
_____
_____
_____
_____

Give us leaders who will keep us from the worship of other gods.

▶▶ Pray & Declare ◀◀

_____

_____

_____

_____

_____

_____

_____

_____

_____

_____

_____

_____

_____

Restore our fathers who will teach, cover and protect our homes. Cause our men to arise and lead our families into generational restoration.

>> Pray & Declare <<

_____

_____

_____

_____

_____

_____

_____

_____

_____

_____

_____

_____

_____

_____

Restore true strength to our women who have been forced to take the reins of leadership because of father-absence. Keep them strong, Lord, as they rest in the strength of the men You are restoring this day.

》》 Pray & Declare 《《

_____

_____

_____

_____

_____

_____

_____

_____

_____

_____

_____

_____

Restore the stolen, identity-ripped, raped, stripped and molested due to our disobedience. Remove the deceptions, lies and fabrications that have stripped our sons and daughters of true identity.

⟫⟫ **Pray & Declare** ⟪⟪

_____

_____

_____

_____

_____

_____

_____

_____

_____

_____

_____

_____

_____

THE RETURN OF A PEOPLE
PART THREE

Abba (Father), we return to You humbled, seeking Your face and turning from our wicked ways. Forgive us Lord (Yah), and heal our land, even to all the land we have been scattered.

>> **Pray & Declare** <<

_____

_____

_____

_____

_____

_____

_____

_____

_____

_____

_____

Our fathers saw with their own eyes the great things You did in Egypt to Pharaoh and his servants, and also to the land itself. They witnessed first-hand the signs, miracles and wonders that baffled the first Egyptian Hamitic enslavers. Yet in our day we have not had the understanding of heart, neither eyes to see or ears to hear attentively, until now.

》》 Pray & Declare 《《

_____

_____

_____

_____

_____

_____

_____

_____

_____

_____

_____

_____

_____

Father, open the eyes of our hearts so that we may see and understand. Open our ears to hear with intention.

Pray & Declare

We have heard of Your mighty works, Most High, but we ourselves have not seen them. We now ask You to reveal them to us in this day.

⟫ Pray & Declare ⟪

_____

_____

_____

_____

_____

_____

_____

_____

_____

_____

_____

_____

We understand and declare Your unending mercy, fully operative grace, and Your unconditional, undying, never-failing love for us, Your chosen people.

>> Pray & Declare <<

_____

_____

_____

_____

_____

_____

_____

_____

_____

_____

_____

_____

Abba, our fathers saw without understanding, perception or attentiveness, and they therefore didn't grasp the greatness of Your love for us, Your people. They made too common Your goodness.

>> Pray & Declare <<

_____
_____
_____
_____
_____
_____
_____
_____
_____
_____
_____
_____

They walked away from You, but we return as a remnant for the entirety of Your people. Heal our entire nation, which You have scattered to the four corners of the earth.

Pray & Declare

_____

_____

_____

_____

_____

_____

_____

_____

_____

_____

_____

_____

_____

Bring us, oh God, to understanding of heart so that we never, ever return to this mental state again--seeing but not seeing, and hearing but not hearing.

>> Pray & Declare <<

_____

_____

_____

_____

_____

_____

_____

_____

_____

_____

_____

_____

_____

Father, be gracious unto us and permeate our minds and hearts to know You, and not just hear of You.

》》 Pray & Declare 《《

_____

_____

_____

_____

_____

_____

_____

_____

_____

_____

_____

_____

Lord, these 400 years of being enslaved, mistreated and humbled have been gruesome, but we are still here.

 Pray & Declare

_____

_____

_____

_____

_____

_____

_____

_____

_____

_____

_____

Many of us prosper; others carry great influence, and the nations of the earth still follow and duplicate our grace, but we ourselves have not collectively recognized Your goodness to us as a chosen people.

》》 Pray & Declare 《《

_____
_____
_____
_____
_____
_____
_____
_____
_____
_____
_____

Our mindset is void of understanding, depleted of substance and absent to opportunity. We fight and protest as people entitled to low-level existence, not as the chosen people. Restore us, oh God, and reset original intent into our psyche.

》》 Pray & Declare 《《

_____

_____

_____

_____

_____

_____

_____

_____

_____

_____

_____

_____

_____

We've allowed the trap of evil, Babylonian propaganda and bigotry to hold our hands and maintain a grip on our minds. Our eyes have been blinded by glaring promises that never manifest.

>>> Pray & Declare <<<

_____

_____

_____

_____

_____

_____

_____

_____

_____

_____

_____

_____

Our politicians fight for their pockets and not Your people, deceived by party partisanship-- just as our forefathers were blind to see, and deaf to hear, while in the section 8 housing of Goshen in the land of Mizraim. Moses went to deliver them, but they refused deliverance, though the bands of bondage were loosed from them.

》》 Pray & Declare 《《

_____

_____

_____

_____

_____

_____

_____

_____

_____

_____

_____

Restore us, oh God. Reset original intent into our psyche. We ourselves harm each other, yet we cry in protest and demand that our lives matter. However, by our acts we demonstrate that they should matter to everyone but us.

▶▶ Pray & Declare ◀◀

_____

_____

_____

_____

_____

_____

_____

_____

_____

_____

_____

We have embraced the demagogic style of self-proclaimed leaders among us, whose bottom line is personal gain maintained through the on-going suffering of Your people.

Pray & Declare

_____

_____

_____

_____

_____

_____

_____

_____

_____

_____

_____

We love not ourselves nor each other, but we fight for everyone else as we shatter in demise. Lord we repent and turn back to You and Your way. Restore us, oh God, reset original intent into our psyche.

>> **Pray & Declare** <<

_____

_____

_____

_____

_____

_____

_____

_____

_____

_____

_____

Make clear again Your heart and voice to those You have made as prophets in the earth--prophets who arise beyond "churchianity" and religious dogma, and into industry, marketplace and political influence.

⟫ Pray & Declare ⟪

_____

_____

_____

_____

_____

_____

_____

_____

_____

_____

_____

_____

_____

Give us leadership who will declare and decree Your heart and thoughts regarding Your chosen--free of the limiting actions of opinion, paradigm and propaganda influence. Open our eyes to only see-to-speak what You show and say.

⟫ Pray & Declare ⟪

_____

_____

_____

_____

_____

_____

_____

_____

_____

_____

_____

_____

By the covenant You have already cut with us and secured in Jesus, re-establish us now as Your people. Be our Elohim (God) as You promised us when You swore to our fathers Abraham, Isaac and Jacob, for we return to You, Most High. This covenant was not limited to us, but to whoever stands with us before the Lord our God.

》》 Pray & Declare 《《

_____

_____

_____

_____

_____

_____

_____

_____

_____

_____

_____

_____

_____

Four-hundred years we have lived in this land of bondage and slavery, yet a land contrasted with great liberty and freedom. We have embraced detestable things and have also kneeled to idolatrous worship packaged in deception and partial truth.

Pray & Declare

_____
_____
_____
_____
_____
_____
_____
_____
_____
_____
_____
_____
_____

We accepted a gospel that emotionalized us, anesthetizing generations into dependency and deprivation. Lord, we repent and turn back to You and Your way. Restore us, oh God, reset original intent into our psyche, transform us as we renew our minds.

Pray & Declare

_____

_____

_____

_____

_____

_____

_____

_____

_____

_____

_____

_____

THE RETURN OF A PEOPLE
PART FOUR

Even now, Lord (Yah), we are aware that many are yet bound to the wickedness of deceit. They perpetuate themselves as Your voice to Your people, deem themselves exempt of living the life You desire, holy and acceptable, and ruin the lives of others with their emotionally polarizing ways.

⟩⟩ Pray & Declare ⟨⟨

_____

_____

_____

_____

_____

_____

_____

_____

_____

_____

_____

_____

Arise, Lord of Hosts, and don't let deceivers off the hook, but expose clearly and precisely the intent of their hearts so that they may repent, process and change. If they do not repent, destroy them with the same curses of the book of the law, which they use to manipulate for personal gain.

>> Pray & Declare <<

_____

_____

_____

_____

_____

_____

_____

_____

_____

_____

_____

_____

Weed out all roots that bear poisonous and bitter fruit--those who hear Your covenant and bless themselves in the wickedness of heart, believing they are safe, though they walk in stubbornness of heart. Let Your anger and jealousy smite against them, and let the curses of this book settle upon their ways and blot out their names here in the earth.

⟫ Pray & Declare ⟪

_____

_____

_____

_____

_____

_____

_____

_____

_____

_____

_____

Just as the spirit of Achan arose in the days of Joshua, we commit to the memorializing of all who posture Your people into being defeated because of their disobedience and greed. May their days of misrepresentation, manipulation and greed be shortened upon the earth.

▶▶ Pray & Declare ◀◀

_____
_____
_____
_____
_____
_____
_____
_____
_____
_____
_____
_____

We ask that You immediately activate the Joshuas and Calebs of our day who have followed Your way without guile of heart and Absalom-like intentions.

>> **Pray & Declare** <<

_____

_____

_____

_____

_____

_____

_____

_____

_____

_____

_____

_____

_____

We call for Your righteous anger and jealousy to erupt against every media system, destructive agenda and anti-Christ structure. Erupt like a volcano and melt its very present foundation, destroy its structure, eliminate its back-up plan and restore Your people to their highest estate.

Pray & Declare

Lord, we call upon Your mercy as we humble ourselves, seek Your face and turn from our wicked ways. From Your high estate, hear us, forgive us and heal our lands.

》》 Pray & Declare 《《

_____

_____

_____

_____

_____

_____

_____

_____

_____

_____

_____

_____

Even those who misrepresented You in weakness, You know their hearts. Forgive those who come in purity of heart for change; but those who refuse change, though they repent, no longer position them where temptation causes them to lead us, Your people, into a far worse state.

>> Pray & Declare <<

_____
_____
_____
_____
_____
_____
_____
_____
_____
_____
_____
_____

Abba Father, we return! We understand the plagues and sicknesses that have been laid upon the land and the people. We seek not to repeat that cycle of a slave diet, which has resulted in sickness and disease generationally unique to us, Your people.

>> **Pray & Declare** <<

_____

_____

_____

_____

_____

_____

_____

_____

_____

_____

_____

We renounce every self-affliction that would bring brimstone, salt and burning, and eliminate the possibilities of vegetation and fruitfulness in our lands. You did this in Your anger and wrath. We are the last of the generations who have experienced this, and we repent and return to You.

≫ Pray & Declare ≪

_____

_____

_____

_____

_____

_____

_____

_____

_____

_____

_____

_____

Our Doctors shall once again be the envy of all things medical, returning us back to a physical state of wholeness through the medical study of Your anatomical laws.

>> Pray & Declare <<

We thank You for cures to all sicknesses and diseases, and not simply temporary technological fixes rooted in pharmaceutical dependency and witchcraft chemical potions.

⟫ Pray & Declare ⟪

_____

_____

_____

_____

_____

_____

_____

_____

_____

_____

_____

_____

_____

Lord, we pray that our future generations, and the stranger that shall come from a far land, will come and bow to the name of The Lord (Yah) who has delivered us from plagues and sicknesses that once overwhelmed Your people. They will praise You that vegetation grows in dead places--made alive by Your land-healing hand.

⟫⟫ **Pray & Declare** ⟪⟪

_____
_____
_____
_____
_____
_____
_____
_____
_____
_____
_____
_____
_____

Their 400-year testimony will be that our fathers turned back to the All Mighty, and the anger of the Lord was reversed; and that we are recipients of the blessings written in the book of the law, that even future generations of our children will not turn away from.

▶▶ Pray & Declare ◀◀

_____

_____

_____

_____

_____

_____

_____

_____

_____

_____

_____

_____

Abba, our children want and need to see You. They want to know You, and they have resolved that they will follow who they see and know.

⟫ Pray & Declare ⟪

_____

_____

_____

_____

_____

_____

_____

_____

_____

_____

_____

_____

We can no longer rely upon speech to quench our children's thirst or motivation to occupy them, they need signs, miracles and wonders.

»» Pray & Declare ««

_____

_____

_____

_____

_____

_____

_____

_____

_____

_____

_____

_____

We return to operate in Your authority and power, exempting ourselves of religious activity and microwaved solutions.

>> Pray & Declare <<

_____

_____

_____

_____

_____

_____

_____

_____

_____

_____

_____

We are agents and custodians of Your supernatural power manifested, distinguishable and holy. They will know that this is not witchcraft, voodoo, hexes, vexes, psychic and familiar spirit activity, but the authentic and holy power of The Lord (Yah) our Elohim.

>> Pray & Declare <<

_____
_____
_____
_____
_____
_____
_____
_____
_____
_____
_____
_____
_____

Many have heard stories of Your goodness, but now they must see and experience it for themselves. Father, the secret things have been revealed.

>> Pray & Declare <<

_____

_____

_____

_____

_____

_____

_____

_____

_____

_____

_____

_____

With our identity stolen, and after being silenced to secrecy, we take responsibility for our heritage and identity. We, nor our children, will no longer live bound from fully honoring You.

⟫ **Pray & Declare** ⟪

_____

_____

_____

_____

_____

_____

_____

_____

_____

_____

_____

Though we are set free from the curse of the law and are not bound as a cursed people, we choose Your thoughts and Your ways, oh God.

>> Pray & Declare <<

_____

_____

_____

_____

_____

_____

_____

_____

_____

_____

_____

_____

THE RETURN OF A PEOPLE
PART FIVE

Here we are Abba (Father), scattered among the nations, people of the blessings and the curses that You have set before us once again. We now take them to heart and repent, we and our children return to You Lord God (Yah Elohim) to obey You with all our heart and soul.

>> Pray & Declare <<

_____

_____

_____

_____

_____

_____

_____

_____

_____

_____

_____

_____

_____

You promised to restore our fortunes--all that we have lost-- and You would have compassion on us. You promised to gather us again from all the nations where You have scattered us.

>> **Pray & Declare** <<

No matter where we end up, You promised You would get us out and bring us back to the land our ancestors possessed, and it will be ours again.

>> **Pray & Declare** <<

_____

_____

_____

_____

_____

_____

_____

_____

_____

_____

_____

_____

You promised to restore unto us a good life and make us more numerous than our ancestors.

Pray & Declare

Cut away the callousness of our hearts and our children's hearts. Free us to love You with our whole hearts and souls, and to live abundantly.

>> Pray & Declare <<

_____
_____
_____
_____
_____
_____
_____
_____
_____
_____
_____
_____
_____

Do a divine reprogramming of our human hearts. Inscribe your laws upon our hearts, but even greater, instill in us Your love-- acting loyally and honoring our commitments.

》》 Pray & Declare 《《

_____

_____

_____

_____

_____

_____

_____

_____

_____

_____

_____

_____

Because of the sacrifice of Jesus (Yahusha, Yeshua), our Kinsman Redeemer, we ask that You show mercy upon our enemies who have hated us, but dismantle their forces, and strip them of all effectiveness. Make them to know that You have loved us with an undying love, and that You are the God who restores.

》》 Pray & Declare 《《

_____
_____
_____
_____
_____
_____
_____
_____
_____
_____
_____
_____

We thank You for a fresh start as we observe to do Your commands.

Pray & Declare

_____

_____

_____

_____

_____

_____

_____

_____

_____

_____

_____

_____

_____

So Father, as You have
promised, blow our minds
and outdo Yourself in causing
things to go well for us as we
prosper in every area of our lives.

▶▶ **Pray & Declare** ◀◀

_____

_____

_____

_____

_____

_____

_____

_____

_____

_____

_____

_____

Our babies will not be aborted, but full-term, healthy and strong.

>> Pray & Declare <<

_____

_____

_____

_____

_____

_____

_____

_____

_____

_____

_____

_____

_____

Our food will not be destructive to our bodies, and we will adhere to Your diet--growing crops and fruits nutritional to our bodies. Our livestock will produce fruit and nurture the ground.

⟫ Pray & Declare ⟪

_____

_____

_____

_____

_____

_____

_____

_____

_____

_____

_____

_____

Lord, You said that You would again take delight in prospering we, Your people, as You did our fathers. We believe You, and trust in Your word.

>> Pray & Declare <<

_____
_____
_____
_____
_____
_____
_____
_____
_____
_____
_____
_____
_____

We will obey Your voice, oh Lord, our God, and keep the commandments and statutes that are written in the Book of the Law, but more-so that which is written upon our hearts. We will turn back to You continually, Most High, with all of our heart and soul.

>> **Pray & Declare** <<

_____

_____

_____

_____

_____

_____

_____

_____

_____

_____

_____

_____

Hear this prayer, Father--the prayer of a people who are turning back to You. You said that You would hear us when we turn back to You, and here we are--turning back to You.

>> Pray & Declare <<

_____

_____

_____

_____

_____

_____

_____

_____

_____

_____

_____

_____

_____

We understand that the given commands are not unreachable or far off, and that Your grace is sufficient for us all to walk in Your way.

>> Pray & Declare <<

_____

_____

_____

_____

_____

_____

_____

_____

_____

_____

_____

_____

Your Word is in our mouthes and in our hearts, so that we can do it. We also know that death and life are in the power of the tongue, and we will either have death as our fruit, or produce the abundant life Jesus came to provide us.

>>> Pray & Declare <<<

_____

_____

_____

_____

_____

_____

_____

_____

_____

_____

_____

_____

So, give us divine wisdom. Remove the limitations of human knowledge so that we will know You. For with You, nothing shall ever be impossible.

>> Pray & Declare <<

_____

_____

_____

_____

_____

_____

_____

_____

_____

_____

_____

_____

Today You have set in front of us the choice of life and prosperity, or death and adversity. We choose life and prosperity. Prosper us, oh God, for we are Your people, and we return unto You now and throughout all millennia.

▶▶ **Pray & Declare** ◀◀

In order for us to live, thrive, increase and multiply, we set our hearts and souls to love you, Lord God (Yah Elohim). This love means to act loyally, and honor our commitment to the agreement You have made with us this day.

>>> **Pray & Declare** <<<

_____

_____

_____

_____

_____

_____

_____

_____

_____

_____

_____

_____

Bless us in this land, and the land we are about to enter and possess.

Pray & Declare

_____

_____

_____

_____

_____

_____

_____

_____

_____

_____

_____

_____

_____

THE RETURN OF A PEOPLE
PART SIX

If the hearts of the people who agree to keep Your commandments, statutes and judgements, turn back to worship other gods and serve them, turn not away from Your people; for the remnant will never cease to walk away.

Pray & Declare

_____
_____
_____
_____
_____
_____
_____
_____
_____
_____
_____
_____

We, Lord, will hold to Your ways and make the testimony of Your judgments as You move against those who refuse to obey Your commandments, statutes and judgements.

⫸ Pray & Declare ⫷

_____
_____
_____
_____
_____
_____
_____
_____
_____
_____
_____
_____
_____

Heaven and earth, hear us this day, and record that God has set before us life and death, blessing and cursing, and we choose life so that we and our seed will live. We thank You, Father, for the options, but we take your advice in choosing life.

》》 Pray & Declare 《《

_____

_____

_____

_____

_____

_____

_____

_____

_____

_____

_____

_____

We choose life in the covenant because we know You are life, and it's by living in covenant that we are able to love You, obey Your voice, and hold fast to You. You are our life and length of days.

⟫ Pray & Declare ⟪

_____

_____

_____

_____

_____

_____

_____

_____

_____

_____

_____

_____

_____

You will make us productive, and we will dwell in the land that You swore to give our fathers Abraham, Issac, and Jacob. We thank You, Lord (Yah), and seal this prayer in the name of Jesus, our Redeemer.

》》 Pray & Declare 《《

_____
_____
_____
_____
_____
_____
_____
_____
_____
_____
_____
_____
_____

AFTERWORD

Prayer: The Key to Freedom for The Black Race

And he said unto Abram, know of a surety that thy seed shall be a stranger in a land that is not theirs, and shall serve them; and they shall afflict them four hundred years; And, that nation, whom they shall serve, will I judge: and afterward shall they come out with great substance.

Genesis 15:13-15

"You know my people are not from here we are from Israel and you know your people are not from America you are from Israel. I just don't know why God did this to us."

Ashanti Supreme Chief to Minister Onleilove Chika Alston June 2018 in Kumasi, Ghana (the capital of the Ashanti Kingdom)

We have marched, we have boycotted, we have voted, we have opened Black-owned businesses, we have broken records and won awards, but have we returned to our maker? Have we returned to The Holy One who married us on Mount Sinai after he freed our Hebrew ancestors from Egyptian slavery, then freed us from Babylonian captivity, Roman domination, and chattel slavery?

I am a faith-based community organizer and advocate who owns multiple businesses, and so everything mentioned above I have done and continue to do. Marching, rallies, voting, Black businesses etc. are all well and good but the fact is that Yahweh, our maker, holds the key to our freedom because HE is the one that allowed us to go into this bondage. After 400 years, we have tried and done many things to obtain full freedom and yet we are still held captive by Post-Traumatic Slave Syndrome, Willie Lynch divisions (even if the letter is not real, what is described in the letter occurs in our communities daily), generational sins, and Africa, which is the richest continent in the world, is still being carved-up and pillaged to make every nation on earth rich but our people.

Apostle B. Dwayne Hardin is truly an Apostolic leader for our people during this hour and his book *The Return of A People* is a landmark work of timely and needed prayers to break the strongholds that keep our people in bondage. When we examine the story of the Exodus, we see that when the groans and cries of the Israelites reached the ears of Yahweh THEN the process of liberation began. In Exodus 2: 23-25, we read:

During that long period, the king of Egypt died. The Israelites groaned in their slavery and cried out, and their cry for help because of their slavery went up Yahweh. Yahweh heard their groaning, and he remembered his covenant with Abraham, with Isaac and with Jacob. **So, Yahweh looked on the Israelites and was concerned about them.**

It was when the cries and groans reached the ears of Yahweh that our Father remembered the covenant he made with our forefathers, and the process of liberation began. Apostle Hardin challenges us to cry out again, to groan even so that the process of our final liberation, The Greater Exodus spoken about in scripture, will occur.

Jeremiah 16:14-15 states:

It shall no longer be said, "As Yahweh lives who brought up the people of Israel out of the land of Egypt," but "As

Yahweh lives who brought up the people of Israel out of the north country and out of all the countries where he had driven them." For I will bring them back to their own land that I gave to their fathers.

Yes, a Greater Exodus is coming. Our people who are being oppressed all over the world will be brought back to our own land to live under the millennial reign of Yahshua our Prophet, Priest and King.

Could it be that if our people embarked upon massive, collective, and personal prayers that this could jumpstart the Greater Exodus?

As someone who has organized against the injustices faced by Blacks in America, I have found that prayer is desperately needed in the struggle for liberation.

A few years ago, as I looked through my Facebook newsfeed, I saw many of my African American friends asking, "How long, oh Lord?" This question was not merely asked after Alton Sterling and Philando Castile were added to the latest victims of racial violence, but it is a question our parents, grandparents, and many generations have asked as they faced oppression.

Police killed at least 136 black people in 2016, according to *The Guardian*'s project The Counted, which tracks police killings in America.

And we were just in the seventh month of 2016.

As I watched the video of Alton Sterling taking his last breath, I thought about the countless Black bodies murdered due to racial violence, and I tweeted this:

My biggest prayer with my entire heart, soul and mind is that my people will be free from this captivity and that my descendants will be free.

Reading Luke 11:1-13, I am reminded of one of the most famous prayers in history: The Lord's Prayer. Prayer was extremely important in the Hebrew culture Yahshua grew up in, which is why out of the many things his disciples could have asked him to teach them, they asked him to teach them to pray.

The Hebrew word *Tefilah* (תפילה) is generally translated in English as the word "prayer", but this is not an accurate translation. "To pray" means to beg, beseech, implore, and the like. *Tefilah* calls us to deep, honest prayer, and not the calm, cool, and collected prayer of a comfortable person. It calls us to the cry of the desperate. Are we as a people desperate for liberation? After Yahshua taught his disciples *what* to pray he taught them *how* to pray with faith and trust that their Heavenly Father will provide them what they asked. This is probably the hardest lesson in prayer because after you sincerely pour out your heart to Yahweh, you must then trust that you will be given what you requested in prayer. Some things are easy to trust Yahweh for but other things, like systematic justice for our people and world peace, are harder to trust you will receive.

So, what do we do? Stop praying? What do we pray? How long, oh Lord, how long do we wait? I am a firm believer in the words of Yahshua's little brother, James the Just: "Faith without action is dead." (James 2:17)

As I desperately cry out to Yahweh for my people to receive justice, I also pray with my feet as I march, and pray with my hands as I organize with leaders rooted in their faith. As a people, we must believe that, ultimately, it is Yahweh who will answer our prayers for justice. We must believe this deep down in our souls—that our prayers and actions are not in vain. I know that believing is easier said than done, but my enslaved ancestors prayed for freedom, and though many of them did not receive it in their lifetimes, I am free from slavery.

The key to praying during times of desperation—when the videos of dead Black bodies do not stop playing on our news feeds, in our minds, and in our souls—is to believe that despite the evil in our world that we serve a good Heavenly Father—one who is just and loving, and whose greatest longing is that justice reign on earth.

I believe that for our prayers to be heard they must be authentic. Yahshua did not teach his disciples to pray to the far away, majestic god, but to "Our Father," which denotes intimacy. For you to be intimate with someone, you must be honest with them. Are we willing to pray honest, desperate prayers for justice? Are we willing to tarry in prayer for justice? Are we willing to pray angry prayers for justice? Are we as a people willing to cry out honestly before Yahweh for justice? If we truly believe He is a God that delights in giving his children justice, then the answer is *yes*.

Remember, when Yahshua taught his disciples to pray, they were poor Hebrew men living under Roman oppression. Yahshua would die much in the same way as Alton Sterling, Philando Castile, and others executed by law enforcement, and with his dead body on display for everyone to see. However, Yahshua rose on the third day, and when he rose, he made it possible for our people to be free!

Now is the time for our people across the world to raise our voices to *tefilah* (pray urgently) for justice—not just with words but with an honest, humble, broken return to our Father—and then the process of our total liberation will begin.

Will you join Apostle B. Dwayne Hardin in crying out to Yahweh for justice—believing that He will not deny His children the good gift of freedom?

Made in the USA
Columbia, SC
13 October 2021

46890993R00087